Quail Getting Started

Carole West
Author, Garden Up Green

Second Edition: June 2015
www.GardenUpGreen.com

Acknowledgements

The Readers

This eBook is dedicated to the readers of Garden Up Green and anyone interested in raising quail in their backyard or homestead. My experience raising quail has been inspired to help others implement a natural environment. Quail are a good alternative backyard bird for gardeners and anyone looking for a self reliant addition to their homestead without a long term commitment. It's my hope you discover the benefits and enjoy this book.

Robert West

Robert is the blessing that God carefully placed in my life years ago.   I'm fortunate to have him by my side encouraging me to think positive and move forward with ideas that inspire my actions. It's a wonderful thing to be married to my soul mate. He is extremely supportive and was the one who encouraged me to write this Book.   To say I'm blessed, would be an understatement.

About The Author

In 2009 we moved our family to the country on a small farm in North Texas. There was something about the quiet that inspired this new lifestyle. I was a stay at home mom and before long the kids grew up, preparing to move on with their own lives. In 2014 I decided to begin a new project, Garden Up Green. The blog allows me to help others beyond our farm through gardening, raising backyard birds and building projects. I'm excited about the future and the opportunities that have blessed this path.

Raising quail was inspired by a luncheon my husband attended. One afternoon he came home raving about this fantastic quail meal; it got me thinking we might want to begin raising these birds on our farm. I acted on that thought and the experience has been positive; this involved learning along the way.

Before getting started I researched breeds, housing options and where to purchase these birds. I was frustrated because most everything involved raising quail in cages without land interaction. I stopped researching and decided to figure things out on my own. The goal was to house quail on the ground level providing a natural environment. I learned a lot and recorded my notes. I realized a getting started guide could help others with similar goals.

This book is for new beginners interested in raising quail in their backyard or homestead. It's my hope this will be a useful interactive guide to getting started. The additional blank pages are for recording your own notes and ideas.

CONTENTS

Quail offer many benefits and hours of enjoyment that sometimes can be overlooked because of their size. When I first began raising quail I knew very little; my previous poultry experience involved chickens and ducks. I wanted to add something new to our farm that was different and I find it interesting my husband's work luncheon became inspiration. Through my experience I discovered quail are perfect for the backyard or homestead; they have brought me hours of enjoyment.

There are four specific reasons to have quail, self reliance, simplicity, backyard bonus and release to nature. These four areas became important and helped me stay focused to learn and share my experience. It's possible you may discover other benefits in addition to this list.

SELF RELIANCE

Game birds normally have less individual personality which can keep you from becoming attached, making them a good option for self reliance. You can raise quail for fresh eggs and meat, they offer several nutritional benefits. Quail are cost effective compared to other poultry or game birds allowing start up cost to be almost half from beginning to end. This can be appealing to those establishing a homestead environment. The startup expense will largely depend on the size of your flock and the housing set up.

SIMPLICITY

Quail are simplistic, you can enjoy raising these birds without the demands other poultry offer. Quail should be raised in captivity; protective housing provides security from ground and sky predators. Unlike chickens most quail will not return to their home at night. With a protected environment this makes it possible to leave them unattended for days at a time with enough food and a good water supply. With the proper set up you won't need someone to check on the birds while you're away. We'll be covering housing and feed in chapters four and five.

BACKYARD BONUS

Quail are quiet compared to other birds like chickens or ducks and your neighbors will appreciate that. I remember my first experience raising chickens the rooster was quieter than our hens. Sometimes we forget hens like to announce themselves after laying an egg and it can be just as disturbing as a rooster and last continuous throughout the day depending on how many hens you have. Quail do make a noise and it sounds like a happy chirp, this is the male mating call. The sound is peaceful, and it never seems to get old; neighbors will think it's an everyday wild bird.

RELEASE TO NATURE

When I was a teenager I lived near a wooded area and occasionally a group of quail would run through our open yard as they traveled back into the woods; that memory is a neat one. Once I began raising the Coturnix I thought about the possibility of raising a native breed I could release. This would be the Bobwhite where I live now. To successfully release they need to be raised on the ground.

In recent years there has been a dramatic decrease in the Texas quail population. Helping increase those numbers seemed like a positive reaction. If this is of interest, you should raise the birds on the ground where they're living in a fenced in grassy space, preferably where they can practice flying. Chapter four will cover this type of housing; it can be expensive to set up but it allows opportunity to expand your flock, observe their instincts, and release.

Notes:

CHAPTER 2 – THE RIGHT QUAIL TO RAISE

The right breed of quail depends on your goal. This could include eggs, meat, bug patrol, and enjoyment. In this chapter I'm going to share the different breeds available from hatcheries and the most common quail breeds for a backyard, farm or homestead. Before choosing a breed you need to find out if there are any restrictions in your state or neighborhood. Sometimes rules are implemented down to the county level and most Wild Game Bird Associations can guide you. There is a list of those associations in chapter thirteen.

COTURNIX QUAIL

The Coturnix quail is originally known as the Japanese quail. They were imported to North America in the late 1800's from Europe and Asia. There are several varieties available and they differ in size and color. These varieties are arranged in sub categories, British Range, Tuxedo, English White, Manchurian Golden and Pharaoh. I started with a combination of Pharaoh, British Range and some English White. Keep in mind some breeders will use different sub category names.

The Pharaoh is the largest of all the Coturnix and the best egg producer. The Coturnix is the hardiest of all quail and the most common for egg and meat production. They mature at six weeks, laying eggs at eight weeks, and they're ready to eat between ten and twelve weeks. Egg production is about 200 eggs the first year. This breed is very common to many online hatcheries and local breeders.

BOBWHITE QUAIL

The Bobwhite is another common breed. They're popular in the eastern and southern part of the United States. This breed has very strong flocking instincts and is a bit larger. It's also known for having flavorful meat. Matures at 16 weeks and the hens normally start laying eggs around 24 weeks during the spring and summer. You can expect about 100 eggs the first year.

CALIFORNIA QUAIL

California quail are common in the North and Southwestern part of the USA. This breed likes to roost in trees which are unique compared to other breeds. This is also the state bird of California. Raising this bird in captivity would involve some research as there might be restrictions against it. Their breeding season is from April – June and egg production is minimal.

MOUNTAIN QUAIL

The Mountain Quail can be found in the mountain areas of the USA. They're instincts are similar to the California and they're a little larger. They tend to be a bit shyer than other breeds making it more of a challenge to establish in captivity. Breeding season is from April – June. A few have kept these birds in captivity but it's not a common choice.

GAMBEL QUAIL

The Gambel is located in the dry regions of southwestern USA and Mexico. Many refer to this breed as the desert quail. They're pretty and have similar coloring to the California quail. It thrives in dry areas where there is an abundance of scrubs. They grow fast and fly at about 3 weeks. Egg production begins when temperatures rise, this can depend on where you live making it difficult to predict egg production.

SCALED QUAIL

Scaled Quail can be found in the grassland and desert areas of the southern and western parts of USA. Breeding season is from April – September and you can expect about 60 eggs a year per female. They can do well in captivity if they have a large flock and a pen with a lot of square footage. They tend to be territorial.

MEARN QUAIL

The Mearn Quail can be found in southern Texas, Arizona and New Mexico. It is the smallest range of quail in the USA. They cling to the mountain areas where oak and juniper trees are in abundance. Their feathers are a camouflage very similar to the Coturnix. This breed does not learn to eat through instinct they have to be fed which could be time consuming if raising from babies in captivity.

STARTER FLOCK RECOMMENDATIONS

Out of all these breeds the best for captivity would be the Coturnix and Bobwhite. These would be the easiest breeds and the hardiest with the most benefits. These breeds are also the most common among online hatcheries and local breeders.

When I began planning my first starter flock I chose the Coturnix quail because they matured fast and they're hardy. This made them a great choice for a new beginner. Now I'm currently raising Bobwhite quail and my experience has been very different. I recommend following my blog, Garden Up Green, you'll find details from my experience with the native breed.

Remember every state has different rules for raising game birds; it would be a good idea to research the rules where you live before choosing a breed.

Notes:

Where do you get your foundation stock? That was my big question when I decided to raise quail. Your available resources will vary depending on the time of year you decide to begin. You need to choose a breed before you search resources. I recommend beginning with baby quail; this will allow you to establish a strong immune system within your flock. Beginners should really start with the Coturnix; they are the least difficult, hardiest and most common among breeders and hatcheries.

If your goal is to raise quail to release then make sure you research in detail the native breeds in your area. Native breeds like the Bobwhite can be a little more difficult to keep healthy.

FINDING BREEDERS

If you're looking for a specific breed you may need to increase your search to uncover resources. The information I'm sharing is mainly for the Coturnix and Bobwhite. I purchased my Coturnix starter flock from a local breeder because I wanted to begin during the off season. For many breeders off season means they're birds are raised indoors under lights to continue egg production. These eggs are then hatched in an incubator. I was able to locate a breeder through craigslist; he was about an hour from my location. The experience was valuable; I received a free facility tour; this started with incubating, hatching, brooders, and full grown quail in cages. It was a neat experience and that story can be found on my blog.

I purchased my Bobwhite starter flock online, in the spring of 2015. I found it difficult to regulate temperature control this time of year. I prefer establishing a quail flock in the months of March and April.

WHAT TO EXPECT FROM BREEDERS

Finding breeders can be a little tricky; my best advice is to search on Craigslist. Don't text, don't email, pick up the phone and engage in conversation. Ask questions to find out if the breeder can fill your order. Breeders normally sell fertilized eggs, newly hatched baby quail or full grown quail. This varies from breeders and so will price, I purchased 25 Coturnix quail babies at $1.50 each. I had to drive an hour to purchase but it was worth it because I learned a lot. Most breeders sell quail in batches of twenty-five or fifty; babies range from a $1 each and full grown $3- $5 each. Prices always vary and I don't recommend dickering. Most breeders will automatically share if they have a discount based on volume of purchase. I have found folks who raise birds to sell work hard at what at they do and deserve the price they're asking.

Never judge a breeder, even if you don't like what you see, observe and learn. If the birds are healthy, ask questions. This is your opportunity to learn from someone else. Everybody has a hidden tip and you only uncover those tips by asking questions. Not everyone is willing to share but for some reason my excitement has a way of getting others to open up.

ONLINE HATCHERIES

You can find game birds, poultry and small specialty hatcheries online. When you order online your birds will be mailed through USPS, they're normally shipped the following day after they hatch. They arrive in a box with a matted straw bed. You'll receive a phone call from the post man in the morning letting you know to come pick up your birds. If you decide to order online make sure you can rescue your birds first thing in the morning, this will allow you to get your quail home and placed in a brooder right away. A brooder is like a nursery for quail.

Prices will vary among hatcheries and many times you can purchase in bulk or prior to hatching season to receive a price break. If fifty or a hundred quail sounds like a lot of birds, then I recommend ordering with a friend. This will allow you to split the order and still receive the discount. Quail are small and once full grown they fit in your hands, so a large quantity of birds isn't that big of a deal.

When I order from a new online hatchery it's best to call before placing the order and ask questions. This will give you an idea of their customer service and if the facility is legit. For me if they don't have time to answer questions they don't get my business. I have run into several rude online hatcheries, when this happens I thank them for their time and move on. I won't do business with establishments that don't have time to answer questions; because if a problem surfaces after the birds arrive they probably won't be willing to help.

HATCHERIES

This is a list of online hatcheries for ordering quail; I used WR Hatchery for my bobwhite quail purchase. They were extremely helpful especially when I ran into difficulties. I haven't used the others and most operate through a seasonal calendar. Hatchery breeding seasons for quail normally begin in May – Sept.

J and M Game Birds: http://www.jandmgamebirds.com
WR Hatchery: http://www.wrhatchery.com/bobwhite
McMurray Hatchery: https://www.mcmurrayhatchery.com
Stromberg Chickens: https://www.strombergschickens.com
Cackle Hatchery: http://www.cacklehatchery.com
Indian Lake Game Bird: http://www.indianlakegamebirds.com
Dunlap Hatchery: https://www.dunlaphatchery.net
B and D Farm: https://bdfarm.com
Signature Poultry: http://www.signaturepoultry.com
Game Bird Farm: http://www.gamebirdfarm.net

To increase your options search online because there might be a hatchery where you live. Your foundation flock is an important purchase and feeling good about where you start will speak volumes towards your experience. Begin the journey with one breed and be prepared before they arrive. Diving in can be fun but not being prepared can mean money wasted. Once you've chosen the breed and where to purchase it's time to begin planning the housing set up. This is where it gets interesting because sometimes we seek what we want instead of what's best for the quail.

Notes:

Once you make the decision to own quail the next step is to choose housing. This will depend on the size of your starter flock; a good rule for proper coop housing is one quail per 1 square foot. Quail should not be overcrowded; they will fight in tight living conditions. The birds should be fully feathered before moving from the brooder to the coop. This will be between 3 or 4 weeks and can vary depending on the breed.

The coop options I'll be sharing have interaction with the ground. This allows for a protected free range environment, safe from predators while allowing their instincts to mature. These coops are not traditional among most quail breeders and I designed them based on green living. Four coop styles are listed in this chapter; they vary according to size and space conditions. I've also enclosed building plans for the mobile quail coop; this design is perfect for smaller flocks in the backyard or homestead.

With these coop designs I used chicken wire and then placed pine fence boards from the base of the frame; this is for protection from predator break in. If you decide to let your quail incubate their own eggs and raise their babies these boards will keep baby quail from escaping. When quail are young they can fit through this wire. The chicken wire allows for bugs to easily get inside so the quail can enjoy a free range diet; they're great foragers.

If you've searched through my blog you will notice a two story coop.   Don't build a two story quail coop – they won't use the second floor because quail prefer to be on the ground all the time.   Remember 1 bird per 1 square foot; you'll find different information online I'm not a believer in overcrowded housing, it's asking for trouble. In chapter nine I talk about disease which almost always brings us back to housing. Put careful attention towards the coop set up; build something you and the quail can enjoy together.

I started my quail in a mobile quail coop; it was a great set up. I wanted something bigger so I moved them into a coop that was 8 ft. x 32 ft x 4ft. This allowed the birds to fly and explore as if they were living in the wild. After a visit to the Dallas zoo I decided to go bigger and established the Sanctuary with my sons help, this set up is my favorite, it measures 60 ft x 12ft. 6 ft.   I also trade a few quail with the Garden Quail Coop, this helps deplete the bugs in my covered raised beds. Let's take a look at these coops to see which one could work best for your space.

The mobile quail coop is an 8 ft. x 4 ft. x 2 ft. frame, allowing you to house up to 20 quail comfortably. It lays flat on the ground so you can move it when necessary; moving the coop provides a clean grass living space. A mobile coop is less expensive to maintain and better for the ground.   There is no purchase of shavings or sand, because the ground and grass is their bedding. You should only need to move your coop about once a week depending on how many quail are in your flock. They'll be able to eat bugs and fertilize while maintaining their natural instincts.   This is a simple frame design with two doors.

This project could easily be completed on a weekend; building plans are available in the last chapter and a video at Garden Up Green on You-Tube will walk you through how to use the mobile quail coop.

QUAIL COOP #2 – THE GARDEN QUAIL COOP

This coop is perfect for gardeners; it involves the covered raised bed. The goal is to have at least three 8 ft. x 4 ft x 2 ft. covered raised beds so you can move the small house to each one when necessary. The house is a simple box design on legs that sits level to the bed frame. Moving the house allows rest time between raised beds, the quail will fertilize during their stay, eat bugs and live as if a regular coop. House up to six or eight quail in this set up because larger quantities may destroy your plants. It's a two part project that might take a little time to complete but you'll love the results.

This set up would be nice to have available and use in conjunction with the Mobile or Stationary coops. Having additional housing allows you to move your birds around to decrease the bug population.   You could use this design as a permanent option as long as you have a small flock and at least three covered raised beds for rotation. To build a covered raised bed frame check out Chapter 15, the mobile quail coop design is very similar. You attach the cover to an existing raised bed using hinges.

QUAIL COOP #3 – STATIONARY COOP OPTIONS

If you have an abundance of space then I recommend large stationary coops. These options let the quail live and fly in a protected environment, where their instincts will mature. These options can also work as a fence divider and coop for those who may have acreage available. This can be a lengthy project depending on the square footage and building could also get pretty expensive. For that reason building in stages is a good alternative. This offers rotational living arrangements each time you add a new section. When you completely finish the coop you can decide to open it as one living space or leave in sections.

This would be similar to rotational grazing. Closing off a section for breeding quail is another option; this area would remain undisturbed allowing you to add food and water.

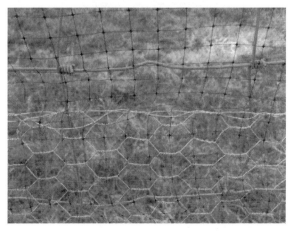

This space is referred to as the sanctuary; it's 60 ft. x 12 ft. x 6 ft. I finished raising my Coturnix quail here; Bobwhite quail live here now. This was an existing structure on our farm that we added a couple seasons ago for a different reason; made from 8 ft. landscaping timbers that went 2 ft. underground connected with 6 ft. 2 x 4's. It's been sitting empty when it occurred to me closing in a section would make a great quail sanctuary. The walls are lined with chicken wire and the roof was enclosed with deer netting. The sanctuary is nice because it's enough square footage for a natural lifestyle. I've added tree branches for hiding, scrubs could also be added for additional shelter. These pictures were taken in the spring and winter; you'll notice the grass is rather high. It's important to cut the grass around the outside of the coop to keep snakes away if that might be a concern where you live. When the space is free of birds I can cut the grass or let my sheep graze.

I recycled an old door for the entrance and we used thin wire to connect the chicken wire to the deer netting. If I were to build this set up from scratch, I would probably build the walls in sections and then connect everything to landscaping timbers. I might also use heavier netting for the roof; the deer netting is working but applying it can be tricky if you live in a windy area.

This next coop is also stationary; this is stage one where I moved the Coturnix quails after the mobile coop lifestyle. This first section measures 8 ft x 16 ft x 4 ft. Later I added the second section which included the same measurements. The walls are covered with chicken wire and the roof is enclosed with deer netting. I have dogs, sheep and llamas that roam my pastures where this coop is stationed and the deer netting would not be a good option for the walls. This coop worked really well, my only dislike is that I couldn't stand up inside. The goal was to keep building expenses to a minimum and that's why a shorter roof was established, 5 ft. or 6 ft. height would have been a better choice.

Keeping the dogs out is always important, I stood by for days with our big dog and any time she had the urge to dig she was disciplined. It took about a week and she connected the quail were not for her.

When the next section was added it connected to the far end and I left the wire in place to offer rotational living spaces. A rotation in smaller square footage also helps decrease risk of parasites.

The travel cage was built so I could transport a few quail to shows. It worked out great and I decided to share the building plans in Chapter fifteen. When the

Coturnix quail were brought to shows many folks were fascinated by these little birds and asked if they could raise quail as pets. I was a little surprised and responded with sure. You need to know that quail have a short life span, wild quail can live up to 2 years and some have reported up to 4 years. This could be difficult for those who get attached to their pets. However knowing that up front can be helpful and requires less of a long term commitment.

The travel cage would make a comfortable home for about 3 quail. If you wanted more space just modify the measurements. It's lined with a removable plastic liner for quick cage cleaning. You may also want to make the cage taller so the birds are easier to view.

FOOD AND WATER DISHES

Food dishes are similar to chick containers; make sure to use open rim water dishes. Feed dishes with circular holes can be dangerous to baby quail, they can get stuck inside and have difficulty escaping without assistance. These metal trays are a great option because you can use them when the quail are adults. They're easy to clean and allow the birds to eat without fighting for space; you can purchase at any farm store or online.

I ran into some complications with my Bobwhite chicks the first week. They decided to use their dishes to sleep, which is a concern for disease. I made wooden feed dishes that were not as wide, also allowing less food waste. They were made from scrap wood with wire mesh on the bottom. This was a great solution, they can still get inside but the desire isn't as great.

You can also make feeders using PVC pipe and a drill. This type of feeder would keep the birds out of the food at all times. It may be a little difficult for day old chicks to figure out; I haven't used them but I'm thinking about making a few in the future.

There are several water feeder options for baby quail, I like the ones with open rims; they're easy to clean and use. Baby quail are small; it's important to add marbles or pebbles to the rim of the water dish, this will keep them from drowning. I started with small water containers when they were in the brooder and then moved to the larger 1 gallon containers once the quail moved outdoors. These containers can be purchased at a farm/feed store or online. Tractor supply is a great source and they're expanding locations.

When quail reach adults switch over to the larger two gallon water containers; make sure food and water feeders are always clean, dirty containers are a welcome to disease. Once the quail reach maturity the marbles are no longer needed.

Notes:

SHELTER BOXES

Quail prefer to lay their eggs on the ground in tall grass or in a small hay pile. They have this camouflage instinct so don't bother with nesting boxes they won't use them. I learned this the hard way after spending hours building nesting boxes. Later I discovered a simple shelter box was a better idea. The quail will use these shelters for shade against hot temperatures, heavy rain, and freezing temperatures.

I found these boxes to be a better option for shelter and their easy to build; they were made from left over wood scrap which means no additional expense. You can move them around the stationary and mobile coops to provide a clean space after occupancy. We receive heavy rains in Texas and these boxes were an added blessing to keep the quail on dry land.

CHAPTER 5 – A QUAIL DIET

The following diet tips are based on the age of the bird. This information can be used as a guide to help establish good health for your quail at the different stages.

HATCHED BABY QUAIL

Introduce baby quail to non medicated wild game feed starter. The brand you choose is a personal choice and most feed stores sell in forty or fifty pound bags; if you can't find a game starter substitute with a high quality dry cat food. Protein needs to be 30% or higher and you'll need to grind it using a blender until it looks like very small bread crumbs. You can also feed baby quail hard boiled chicken eggs. Peel off the shell and mash the egg into small pieces, keep in mind the pieces need to be micro sized, served in small amounts as eggs spoil quickly. Do not leave uneaten eggs in the brooder for more than an hour or two if you choose this option.

After they're a week old and if you haven't experienced any complications you can introduce fruit. Favorites are apples, oranges, pears and peaches, and berries. Make sure to cut and serve the fruit in small amounts; this is a treat in addition with their regular feed. I would recommend fruit twice a week.
At two weeks you may want to introduce meal worms as a treat. This will get them ready for their outdoor home where they'll have access to bugs.

For a healthy clean water supply use chick starter water containers; add pebbles or marbles to the rim; this will keep the birds from drowning. You could also use plastic peanut butter jar lids and add marbles. You will need to clean these dishes about three or four times a day. Quail are messy!

Above: Bobwhite Quail chicks at two days, notice the marbles in their water dish. Below: Coturnix Quail, they're about 1 week old.

At three to four weeks old you can safely put the quail outdoors in their coop. You want your birds to be fully feathered before heading outdoors; their feathers keep them dry and warm. I wanted my quail on a free range diet; bugs and grass grain were their food of choice after they went outdoors. I continued feeding the game feed along with a few fruit treats until they reached maturity. At about five to six weeks I decreased the feed and allowed free ranging as their primary diet, this decision was based on their actions. I also continue to share fruit as a treat.

If you're raising birds off the ground you could gather bugs or purchase meal worms. Implementing a natural diet is important especially if you're raising them to release later. At this age you no longer have to keep marbles or pebbles in their water dish.

FULL GROWN QUAIL

When the quail are older than eight weeks you can expect egg production from the Coturnix breed; they will lay about an egg a day until fall or when daylight hours begin to decrease.

They will be seeking bugs as part of their diet and you can continue with feed and fruit. At this age you no longer need to keep marbles or pebbles in their water dish and you may want to switch to a larger water system, quail can be thirsty little birds; they tend to drink water during the morning and evening.

FOOD TREATS

Fruit is a great treat; they can eat apples, pears, peaches, oranges and berries, chopped in small pieces. Expand their treats with all types of sprouts, small bits of corn on the cob, bird seed mixture, and meal worms. Feed in small doses as these quail don't eat as much compared to other poultry. A little bit of food goes a long way.

Notes:

BREEDING

Once your quail mature decide if you want to increase the flock, by incubating naturally or with an incubator. Males are active and can get aggressive; it's important not to have more males than females in your flock. Five or six females per male are a good recommendation.

Sexing your birds is as easy as holding them upside down and examining the cloaca; this would be underneath the tale. Males will have a small bulge or a release of foam, females will not. Females will also have a loss of feathers on their forehead because the males are rather aggressive during mating.

A couple weeks after the females begin laying eggs you can begin incubating. Many times there can be several broody female quail within your flock. A broody quail is when they sit on the nest of eggs until they hatch. To find out if you have broody quail you need to observe your bird's activity. Watch to see quail sitting on a nest for several days. Sometimes quail will brood in pairs, leave their nest undisturbed. If a broody quail senses their nest is threatened they will leave and relocate; unfortunately broody quail see their caretakers as a threat.

If you choose to let your quail incubate decide if you plan to leave the babies with the quail to raise or pull them and place in a brooder. The mother will raise them if you leave them beside her; add a water dish with marbles and starter feed nearby after they hatch. Do not interfere with the process unless you absolutely have to, sometimes a quail can die after they hatch, and this would be the only time to interfere for removal. Birds are blessed with instincts and it's important to let them alone.

If you're raising a native breed to release back to nature then let the mom take care of them on her own.

Many breeders prefer to grow their flock using the incubation process. Incubators are available online, designed for personal and commercial use. Commercial incubators would be an option if you're looking to turn your quail experience into a business or wanting to raise quail on a larger scale. Incubators can also be purchased at your local farm/feed store. Small farm stores tend to be more knowledgeable. In Chapter thirteen you'll find links for suppliers.

HATCHING WITH AN INCUBATOR

There are a few things to remember when incubating quail eggs; the humidity level is important for successful hatching. Eggs should have 70% humidity during hatching, after the eggs have hatched 80% humidity. The temperature of the incubator should be at approximately 100 degrees during the incubation period prior to hatching.

Carefully set the quail eggs into the incubator when the temperature is correct, the small end of the quail egg should be pointing down. If you're not using an automatic egg turner then turn eggs by hand at 30 degree intervals 3 times a day. This keeps the embryos from sticking and growing to the side of the egg. Stop turning eggs 4 days prior to your scheduled hatch date.

The incubating period depends mainly on the breed. For Bobwhite you're looking at 24 days and Coturnix 17 days. You might have to add a day because some baby quail like to take their time.

BROODER

Once the quail hatch they need to be placed in a brooder to keep them warm. A brooder is like a nursery for quail. The brooder should be set up a couple days prior to your hatch date. Use a plastic tub because they're durable and easy to clean. Line the bottom of the container with hay; you could also use wood chips and then place feed and water. Please read Chapter five, you will find complete feed instructions for feeding baby quail. Remember to add pebbles or marbles into their water dish to keep them from drowning.

You must have a light to maintain their body temperature; in nature the mother would do this. A standard heat lamp will work with a 100- 250 watt red bulb. Keep the temperature at 90 degrees for at least 4 to 5 days and then slowly decrease temperatures as the quail begin to grow and gain feathers. The red bulb keeps flock pecking to a minimum.

Bedding will need to be changed about every 2 days depending on how many quail you house in one container. Remember to have a lid covering the top because once they start to use their wings they will fly out, this begins at week one; quail are very active. Depending on the number of quail will depend on how many brooders you will need.

I have two types of containers I use for brooders. I prefer the black one because it's a higher quality plastic; you can purchase these tubs at any feed/farm store. The lid was made from scrap wood and chicken wire; it slides and allows you to leave a small opening while changing water and feed. The light sits on top or you can hang it from the ceiling, the birds will go under it when they want to warm up. It's always a good idea to keep the light at one end of the brooder.

This brooder set up was used for my Bobwhite quail, the tubs are from Rubbermaid, they're a little larger and the boards help fill in the gaps. The containers are cleaned every day with this breed. Simply remove the birds into a safe place, remove dirty bedding and wash the plastic tubs with warm soapy water; make sure you scrub them clean. This is when you can also thoroughly clean the water and feed dishes before adding the quail back.   A clean brooder is important to the health of your flock.

CHAPTER 7 – MARKET FOR SELLING

If you decide you want to make additional income selling your quail there are several avenues that might be of interest. It's important to research first to see if there are regulations against your goals. Rules can vary from state to state.

Put together a small business plan to see if this income stream will be worth your time. A simple plan will help you discover if there is a demand for quail. I've listed several income opportunities that may be of interest.

PLACES TO SELL

FARMER'S MARKETS
Many cities have wonderful farmer's markets; this could be a fantastic avenue to reach direct customers. Research options and visit locations to see if this is a good possibility. Eggs and processed meat would probably be your best enterprise at a farmer's market.

TRADE DAY MARKETS
These markets are fun and normally happen the first weekend of the month. This is a matter of spending time researching to see if this could be a possibility and if they have an area where you could sell live birds.

ONLINE
Establish a website to market your product. When you're out and about you can reference your product using business cards. The other option would be is to sell your quail on Craigslist; this is where I found my Coturnix breed. There are many online groups, they can be found on social media like Facebook. Selling online is a matter of knowing your area and doing a little research. When you step into the web your opportunities expand.

TARGET AUDIENCE

RESTAURANTS

Fancier restaurants or catering companies may have an interest in processed quail and eggs. You will make more income from this opportunity if you're able to sell live birds. Selling processed birds to restaurants involves a state certified processing set up. Sometimes you can connect with a local processor at their given price. This fee would be added to the purchase of each processed bird.

FARMERS/HOMESTEADERS

Small Farmer's and Homesteaders may be interested in quail of all ages and fertilized eggs for starting their own flock. This would be a good avenue for helping you get recognized as a local quail breeder.

BACKYARD SUBURBS

We all know chickens have made it to the suburbs so why not quail. There may be an interest in edible eggs, fertilized eggs, birds at all ages, and quail housing. The possibilities are endless.

Marketing is the key to any successful business so if you decide to turn your quail flock into a selling opportunity I would recommend implementing some kind of business plan. Even if this is going to be a hobby business you should have a plan with goals for success. Know your audience and be the best. Always present with integrity and you'll have customers for life.

Notes:

CHAPTER 8 – QUAIL IN THE GARDEN

The sound of quail in the garden adds a sense of enjoyment. Quail can be a great fit for gardeners and backyard homesteaders. They make excellent companions, the time commitment is minimal and they're a good option for those with limited space. They can also help deplete the bug population in your garden.

Providing a natural environment like I shared in chapter four is ideal because you experience the best this bird has to offer with little effort. Everybody benefits including your garden.

THE BENEFITS TO QUAIL VERSES OTHER POULTRY

QUIETER

Quail are quieter than traditional poultry and other game birds; your neighbors will appreciate that. They make a chirp sound that is pleasant and sweet; many times people hear them it's referred to as a local wild bird.

EGGS

Fresh eggs, they're smaller but the nutrients are grand. The nutrition base for one egg is: Calories 14, total Fat 1g, Cholesterol 76 mg, Sodium 13 mg, Potassium 12 mg, and Protein 1.2g. Three to four quail eggs equal one chicken egg and I've had a wonderful experience baking and cooking with quail eggs. I recently took six quail eggs and fried them. Cook time was quick and they tasted wonderful. Enjoy these eggs scrambled, boiled and pickled.

MEAT

The Coturnix breed is ready for meat processing between 10 – 12 weeks. Processing is a breeze and what a treat for special guests. Quail is a healthy alternative to your diet, serve a couple baked quail with a few sides and you have a wonderful meal. There are some good tutorial videos on You Tube that will show you how to process quail. I have one linked on my You Tube page.

MATURE FASTER

Most female quail mature at six weeks and lay eggs at eight. When you compare this time frame to chickens that's pretty amazing; chickens normally don't start laying eggs until they're five or six months old.

EAT LESS

You will spend less money on feed because quail don't eat as much as other poultry. Quail enjoy eating bugs, if you house them naturally on the ground this will help supplement their diet and feed expenses.

REQUIRE LESS ATTENTION

Quail can be left for days at a time as long as they have plenty of food and water available. This is great news; a little freedom from the homestead is important.

START UP COST IS LESS

Start up fees will vary with any project; this will be based on the size of your flock. A quail brooder and house set up will normally be a lower expense as the space needed is not as grand. Quail themselves are inexpensive making it less of a commitment when purchasing your starter flock.

BUG PATROL

Quail provide bug patrol in the garden if you house them in that area, you'll want to read chapter four as I cover this in detail. They seem to really enjoy crickets and grasshoppers the most.

How you set up your quail home will depend on the benefits you want available. I'm thrilled with our Quail Sanctuary because it has allowed for all these benefits I've listed to be present. Take time to carefully plan so that you can experience the positive aspects quail have to offer.

Notes:

Disease can arrive when you raise any kind of bird. The overall solution to establishing a disease free environment for your birds is to provide a large set up or use a rotational space. It's very important not to over crowd your birds living conditions and keep things clean. This includes feed and water dishes along with any type of nesting material you may use. Due to the parasite issues listed below many quail owners have decided to raise their birds in a more controlled environment that involves wire cages. This was not my method of choice because I believe a natural environment without overcrowding is a better way to establish a healthy flock.

If parasite and disease are a big concern I recommend de-worming your birds. Products can be purchased online or at your local feed store and you can find tutorials on You Tube. I do not medicate nor do I worm my quail; this is a personal choice. I have found that with a clean environment there are fewer concerns with parasites. I did learn there are exceptions to that statement.

In Texas we experienced a massive decrease in the quail population dating back to 2010. Texas Tech University received grant funds to research the cause and they came up with a parasitic eye worm. I experienced this parasite with one of my Coturnix quail and because I didn't catch in the beginning I chose to put it down. This eye worm is contracted through crickets, not all are a carrier and you shouldn't allow this to keep you from free ranging your birds. The parasite blinds the quail so it fails to escape when predators arrive. It's been stated by the university the effects of this parasite have had a large impact on the quail decline in Texas. There are other diseases to be aware of.

ULCERATIVE ENTERITIS ALSO KNOWN AS QUAIL DISEASE

This disease is caused by a bacterium found in the intestinal tract; contracted by overcrowded housing where the birds ingest contaminated droppings. Once disease is contracted mortality will occur within 5 – 14 days and the ground can be contaminated for a long period of time. Treatment varies because of the size of the bird. Keeping a clean environment using rotated space is a good practice. If you have infected areas let that space sit bird free and clean it up.

Replace all bedding and spray down the surface with water. That area should rest bird free for at least 2 weeks after you clean.

COCCIDIOSIS

This is an internal parasite that affects the digestive system. It normally attacks birds between 2-6 weeks. The parasite is most common with birds that are raised on the ground. Once contracted the birds stop eating and become weak, difficult time standing and become pale. They will die if not treated.

Prevention is what you want to focus on and this goes back to keeping a clean environment for your birds. You don't want a buildup of droppings around the water and food area. A simple solution is to move and clean their dishes every time you feed. Keeping a clean environment will help develop immunity in your flock without experiencing the loss of birds.

HISTOMONIASIS

This is also known as Blackhead and it's a protozoan disease found in fowl and causes mortality in game birds. It's known as the cecal worm which is another parasite; it enters the bird's body as an egg. After entering the bird they relocate to the liver where liver damage begins.

Affected birds will become weak, loss of appetite, and have sulfur colored droppings. It's important to maintain single species flocks as this is more common among hybrid flocks.

CAPILLARY WORMS

This is a digestive parasite worm that enters the system and appears to have a thread like existence. This parasite will eventually starve the bird making it difficult for the bird to breath and it will end up dying if not treated. Prevention would be to worm your birds and ensure for a clean environment.

Note: I have only experienced the parasitic eye worm with one of my quail. I have not experienced any of these diseases I've listed; I do find it interesting the common ground with disease is based on environment. Keeping things clean from the time your birds are babies will help establish a strong immune system for a healthier flock.

Notes:

Showing quail at the fair is a personal choice and one you'll have to do a little research. It's pretty simple and it just takes a phone call to the local 4H or FFA office. They will know if quail are welcome and they'll put you in touch with the right folks. Most organizations will have selected groups at the county level based around specific interests.

Showing at fair can be a great experience for your children. I remember when our kids did fair before we raised any kind of farm animal. One enjoyed it more than the other so it really depends on the project and interest of the child before diving in.

Some fairs allow adults to enter their projects so if this is an avenue you want to pursue with quail get the information first because things will vary from county to state fairs across the country. Sometimes specific rules and recommendations are required prior to participation.

Notes:

Game bird associations are geared more towards the hunter but they can also be a great resource for information. I'm sharing a few that I found online and I'll also add them to Chapter thirteen where you can find many helpful links. You may want to do additional research to see if there are any local associations available in your area. Sometimes connecting with others who have similar interests offline can be a great avenue for learning and making new friends.

Quail Forever: http://www.quailforever.org/
Quail Unlimited: http://www.qu.org/
Texas Wildlife Association: http://www.texas-wildlife.org/
Quail Tech Alliance: http://www.quail-tech.org/

Notes:

The future of quail looks bright, especially for those interested in raising them. Quail are a realistic alternative to chickens or ducks; they offer the same benefits on a smaller scale. If you choose to raise a native breed you can easily release into an open field if you decide you no longer want to continue. That is a beautiful thing!

The parasite concerns in the wild will not end. University researchers are narrowing down the cause while looking for a way to reverse the decline. Helping repopulate the cycle of quail is a simple task and something anybody can help with, you just need to make the decision to do it.

When I first heard about the quail decline it caught my attention. Reading inspired me to become proactive. I believe everything starts at home and we have a responsibility to educate ourselves the best way possible. Learning to care for the environment in which we live really isn't that difficult.

I knew in time I wanted to raise Bobwhite quail after my Coturnix experience. The goal with the Bobwhite would be to establish a flock for ourselves and release the rest.

At our farm we decided in the beginning to raise all of our animals in a natural environment. We carry this concept throughout our land and home and the results have been amazing. I encourage you to do the same and perhaps the future of quail and all wild game birds will look a little brighter.

Learning about the habitat helps you become a better steward of the land, this is why I like raising the birds on the ground and this can happen right in your backyard.

Notes:

QUAIL BREED VISUAL PHOTO LINKS

Coturnix: https://en.wikipedia.org/wiki/Japanese_quail
Bobwhite: https://en.wikipedia.org/wiki/Colinus
California: https://en.wikipedia.org/wiki/California_quail
Mountain: https://en.wikipedia.org/wiki/Mountain_quail
Gambel: https://en.wikipedia.org/wiki/Gambel%27s_quail
Scaled: https://en.wikipedia.org/wiki/Scaled_quail
Mearns: https://en.wikipedia.org/wiki/Montezuma_quail

HATCHERIES

J & M Game birds: http://www.jandmgamebirds.com/
WR Hatchery: http://www.wrhatchery.com/bobwhite
McMurray Hatchery: https://www.mcmurrayhatchery.com
Stromberg's: https://www.strombergschickens.com
Cackle Hatchery: http://www.cacklehatchery.com
Indian Lake Game Birds: http://www.indianlakegamebirds.com
Dunlap Hatchery: https://www.dunlaphatchery.net
B & D Game Farm: https://bdfarm.com/
Signature Poultry: http://www.signaturepoultry.com
CM Game Bird Farm: http://www.gamebirdfarm.net

PURCHASING QUAIL

Craigslist: http://craigslist.org
Canton Trade Days in the Alley: http://firstmondaycanton.com/

INCUBATING SUPPLIES

Brinsea Products: http://www.brinsea.com/
Stromberg's: http://strombergschickens.com
Incubator Warehouse: http://incubatorwarehouse.com
Tractor Supply: http://tractorsupply.com

GENERAL QUAIL SUPPLIES

Quail Supply: http://www.quailsupply.com/
Game Bird Netting: http://3tproducts.com
Cutler's Supplies: http://www.cutlersupply.com

ORGANIZATIONS

Quail Forever: http://www.quailforever.org/
Quail Unlimited: http://www.qu.org/
Texas Wildlife Association: http://www.texas-wildlife.org/
Quail Tech Alliance: http://www.quail-tech.org/

4H & FFA ORGANIZATIONS

National 4H: http://www.4-h.org/
Texas State 4H: http://texas4-h.tamu.edu/
National FFA: https://www.ffa.org/Pages/default.aspx
Texas State FFA: https://www.texasffa.org/

GARDEN UP GREEN ONLINE

Website: http://gardenupgreen.com
Pinterest: http://pinterest.com/gardenupgreen
Google+: https://plus.google.com/+CaroleWest/posts

Notes:

CHAPTER 14 – THE GETTING STARTED CHECKLIST

Use this checklist to help get you stay on the right track. The following list has been assembled in order of importance.

CHECKLIST

1. Choose your breed; newbie's should begin with the Coturnix, they're hardy and mature faster. I recommend starting with baby quail to establish a healthy flock. Chapter 2 and 3 cover breeds, foundation flock.

2. Pick the breed and get your brooder set up. Use Chapter 6 as a guide, total number of brooders will be based on the number of quail you purchase.

3. Decide type of quail coop to establish. Chapter 4 will help you plan and building plans are available in Chapter 13. In three to four weeks your quail need to move outdoors.

4. Once the brooder is established purchase feed, food and dishes. This should all be in place prior to your birds arriving. Revisit Chapter 5.

5. You've made your bird purchase and they've arrived. Place each quail carefully into the brooder. Clean the brooder as needed, I recommend every day the first week and don't forget your quail coop needs to be planned and ready in 3 weeks.

6. Feed when necessary and make sure their water and food dishes are always clean. Provide a clean brooder by changing their bedding every two days. The cleaner their environment the healthier your quail will be.

7. At week three or four it's time to move your birds outdoors into their new home. This is exciting. Put thought in to their permanent home before diving in. Establishing a natural environment is my best recommendation especially if you plan to raise native quail to release.

8. If you chose the Coturnix, you'll enjoy eggs by week eight and processing for meat is a personal choice.

9. Most important enjoy and have fun!

Notes:

BUILDING SAFETY TIPS

This project was made from new wood; you could also build with reclaimed. Always wear safety goggles, work gloves and appropriate protective gear when building.

PROJECT SUPPLIES

- Saw – Electric or Manual, I used a Chop Saw and Jigsaw
- Electric drill
- Hammer
- Wire Cutters
- Heavy Duty Staple Gun
- Sandpaper
- 15 Finishing Nails
- 1 small box 2, ¼ in. screws (Deckmate brand is good)
- 1 small box 1. ¼ in. screws (Deckmate)
- Staples or Staple nails
- Eight 2 x 4 x 8 boards
- Two 1 x 2 x 8 boards
- Four 1 x 4 x 8 Boards
- Five 8 ft Pine Fence boards
- 2 ft and 4 ft width Chicken Wire bundles
- Paint or Stain
- Hardware – Includes 2 door handles, 2 door pulls, two door lock hatches, and 4 hinges

PHASE 1 - FRAME ASSEMBLY

Building Tip: Build this project on a flat surface for best results.

STEP A -BEGIN WITH EIGHT 2 X 4 X 8 FT BOARDS

1. Cutting measurements include – four cuts at four feet each, another four cuts at two feet each. The remainder 4 eight foot boards do not need cutting.

2. Assemble on a flat surface and lay out according to the above picture; this will include eight foot walls inside the 4 foot ends.

STEP B - CONNECTING THE CORNERS

1. Drill two pilot holes in each corner as seen in the above left photo; this will keep the wood from splitting when you drill in the screws.

2. When all four corners are connected, build the same shape again.

3. You end up with two rectangles, lying side by side.

STEP C - CONNECTING THE LEGS

1. The next step is to take the 2 foot legs and connect them to each corner of the frame.
2. The long side of the 2 foot legs will face the 4 foot frame end.
3. You're adding two screws one to each side.
4. Drill pilot holes first and then drill screws in place.

Building Tip: It's handy to have two drills during this process, or drill all the holes first and then go back and insert all the screws.

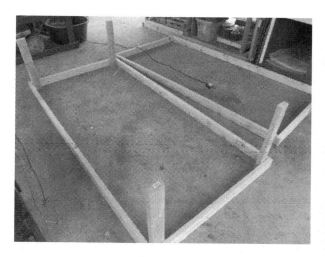 

STEP D - CONNECTING THE FRAME

1. The legs are secure - carefully flip so the frame is standing on its legs inside the other frame, making a rectangle.
2. Repeat the same process for connecting the legs as you did in Step C
3. Frame is secure and connected.
4. Stain or paint your frame and let it dry, this is a good time for a break.

Building Tip: It's easier to paint the frame prior to beginning phase two.

STEP A - CHICKEN WIRE APPLICATION

1. We're covering three open walls with 2 ft. Chicken wire attaching from the inside of frame.

2. Start connecting from one long corner of the frame, leave excess wire at the beginning corner; cut the additional off later.

3. Attach the wire using a heavy duty staple gun or staple nails, you could also use both.

4. Attach the wire from the bottom first and go all the way around the frame.

5. The technique is pull tight and attach, I recommend wearing work gloves.

6. Once the bottom row of wire is attached, connect the corners.

7. The final step is to attach the wire to the opposite long board of the frame, use the pull and attach technique because you want this wire tight.

STEP B – ADD PROTECTIVE BOARDS

1. Take two Pine Fence boards, no cutting necessary.
2. Attach with smaller screws from corner to corner as seen in the above photo.
3. On the closed end add another pine board and cut 3.11 ft – it's a weird measurement so measure that end before you cut the pine boards.
4. Attach this to the bottom as you did the long 8 ft boards.

Building Tip: This application allows younger quail to not escape. The chicken wire allows bugs to jump inside to supplement the quail diet.

STEP C – ADD ROOF WIRE, UPPER DOOR DIVIDER AND PROTECTIVE TRIM BOARDS

On the roof were adding chicken wire and the divider board for the top door. From the corner of the frame measure 2.7 feet towards the center and mark the frame. Then take your other 4 foot board that you had left over from the previous cut and lay that flat across the frame so it's straight. Mark the width of that board, this board will be drill in place after the roof wire is attached.

1. Staple 4 ft roof wire, connect long side first and then attach the short end.
2. Pull the opposite long side of the wire over so it's tight and staple in place.
3. Add the remainder 4 ft pine board on top at the place we marked on the frame. Use two screws on each end.
4. Flip the frame on its side and connect the chicken using a staple gun to the underneath of the pine board. Pull it so it's tight.

5. Turn the coop back over and add the top protective boards using finishing nails.

6. Use two 1 x 2 x 8 boards and cut 5.2 feet – Double check before you cut and gently hammer in place with finishing nails.

7. Use one 1 x 4 x 8 board, cut into 3.9 feet, this will go along the top end. Hammer in place using finishing nails.

Building Tip: When attaching chicken wire, it's a good idea to have an overhang; all excess can be cut off later. It's important for the chicken wire to be tight. Please double check your measurements before cutting the wood. Sometimes if the frame is the least bit off during assembly the rest of the measurements can be off.

BUILD AND ATTACH TOP DOOR

STEP A – BUILDING THE ROOF DOOR

1. Use three 1 x 4 x 8 Boards, saw, drill, small screws,4 ft chicken wire, staple gun and hardware.
2. Cut the outside frame first, you need two 3.11 feet, two 2 feet, and four 1.9 pieces.
3. Lay the door frame on a flat surface and place the corner pieces face down and mark your angle cuts before sawing.
4. Attach each with small screws; a total of sixteen will be needed.
5. Stain or paint the door and then go back and stain or paint the rest of the frame. Once you finish painting the frame this door should be dry enough to add the wire.

STEP B – ADD THE WIRE, HARDWARE AND CONNECT

1. Flip the door so the flat side is facing up and attach the chicken wire with a staple gun.
2. I used my drill to keep the wire roll from rolling forward.
3. Cut off any excess and flip over.
4. Add two hinges and take over to the quail frame.
5. Drill the door to the pine divider board.
6. Add the top door hatch and we're almost finished.

BUILD AND ATTACH END DOOR

STEP A – BUILDING THE END DOOR

1. Use two pine boards cut two pieces at 1.4 feet and three at 3.1 feet.
2. Take one of those 3.1 boards and cut length wise so its width is .5 of a foot.

STEP B – ASSEMBLE THE DOOR

1. Use twelve small screws and attach the boards together as seen in the above photo.
2. Add door handle and hinges.

STEP C – ASSEMBLE DOOR STOP AND ATTACH

1. Cut another pine board at 3.1 feet and screw in place from the inside at the opening.
2. Attach the door to the frame making sure it opens and closes.
3. Add the door handle and Lock hatch.
4. You can stain or paint all the pine boards at this point. Sometimes adding a little color to match your backyard is fun.

Notes:

STEP D – ADD CARRY HANDLES

1. Add the larger carry handles, one or two on each end.
2. The Mobile Quail Coop is finished.

THE SHELTER BOX

This is part of the project is optional; I made it from left over and scrap wood
The Quail like these boxes when it rains, winter cold and shade from the heat.
You can make these boxes to your own size specifications based on how many
quail you will be housing.

Building Tip: On my Blog there is an article, Quail Nesting Boxes. I've
implemented additional styles of shelter boxes you may prefer. Keep in mind
quail nest in the grass they don't use nesting boxes like other birds.

BUILD A SHELTER BOX

STEP A - BUILDING THE SHELTER BOX

1. This frame is 2 x 2 x 1 feet. You need four two foot boards and four 1 foot boards. You can use simple 2 x 4's or 2 x 3 wood pieces to build the frame.
2. This building process is similar to the quail frame; with the exception you skip the bottom frame boards.

STEP B – ADDING THE WALLS, ROOF AND STAIN

1. I used left over pine and 1 x 4 boards to close in the walls with short screws.
2. Added a solid piece of scrap plywood for the roof.
3. Finished the outside of the shelter with stain.

Building Tip: Make these boxes any size you want, remember they need to fit through the roof or end doors.

BUILDING TOOLS

Electric drill, manual or electric saw, hammer, staple gun, wire cutters, measuring tape and protective gear.

BUILDING SUPPLIES

- 2 Eight foot Cedar Fence boards
- 3 Eight Foot 2 x 3's
- Plywood piece for floor
- 24 Screws for Frame
- 10 Screws for attaching the floor
- 44 Short Nails
- Heavy Duty Staples
- Chicken Wire
- 4 Hinges + 2 Handles

FINISHING SUPPLIES

Use sand paper, stain or paint, and heavy duty plastic to line the bottom of the cage. You can use different size wood so I didn't mention the size of nails and screws. Adjust the hardware to your wood choice.

Building Tip: 2 x 3's can be soft and split pretty easy, make sure you always drill pilot holes first and drill slow. I used the smaller wood to keep this project lighter.

STEP ONE

The frame size was a little unique the walls are 3 feet, ends 1.7 and height was 1.3. I was using scrap wood so the measurements are a little strange. You can easily round those numbers off to establish an even project. Cut the wood to size and find a flat surface to work.

Lay your bottom pieces flat so you have two ends and two wall frames; you will be building two sets of these. I pre-drilled and used single screws to assemble each corner together.

STEP TWO

Once the two frames are assembled I added the corner pieces. These were drilled in place using 2 screws, one inserted through each piece of wood. I flipped the structure and attached the other frame the same way making a rectangle.

The next step is to add the bottom piece of plywood using screws and then paint or stain your project before moving on.

STEP THREE

When the frame is dry you can add chicken wire, add to the inside because it looks nice. Attach the wire with a heavy duty staple gun so your wire is secure. Cut off any excess with wire cutters.

STEP FOUR

The cedar fence wood is 8 feet; I took the frame measurements for this step and cut the wood in half down the center. One nail per corner is all you need to keep in place.

STEP FIVE

We need a lid; this is made from cedar fence boards that I cut to size. If you prefer you can buy these boards already cut to size. I nailed the center board in place; this is where the hinges will attach. I then measured the wood according to the open space and cut small corner pieces. These small wood pieces are hammered to keep the door frame functional. I used 4 small nails per corner; once you have a strong door it's now time to flip and add chicken wire with the staple gun. This lid has two flip openings; you can easily modify this step if you prefer a single lid.

STEP SIX

The final steps are connecting the doors with hinges and add the handles so it's easy to transport. It's a good idea to sand the cedar to keep from getting slivers. Line the cage with plastic; a heavy duty plastic garbage bag would work; I lightly laid the plastic in place; fill the bottom with hay and added the birds with food and water.

Final Notes: Clean as needed probably two or three times a week. Quail are messing in confinement; you may want to build bigger if you plan to use this cage for permanent housing indoors.

For more about raising quail visit me online, I'll continue to share my experience beyond Getting Started. www.GardenUpGreen.com

Notes:

Notes:

Disclaimer & Copyright

Made in the USA
Lexington, KY
07 May 2018